Dinner is in a Bag

Fuss-Free En Papillote Recipes

BY

Christina Tosch

Copyright 2021 Christina Tosch

Copyright Notes

This Book may not be reproduced, in part or in whole, without explicit permission and agreement by the Author by any means. This includes but is not limited to print, electronic media, scanning, photocopying or file sharing.

The Author has made every effort to ensure accuracy of information in the Book but assumes no responsibility should personal or commercial damage arise in the case of misinterpretation or misunderstanding. All suggestions, instructions and guidelines expressed in the Book are meant for informational purposes only, and the Reader assumes any and all risk when following said information.

Table of Contents

Introduction 6

Mains 8

    Bacon-Wrapped Rabbit en Papillote 9

    Beef in Parchment with Olive Sauce 11

    Catfish en Papillote 14

    Champagne and Orange Lobster Tails en Papillote 17

    Chateaubriand en Papillote 20

    Clam Spaghetti en Papillote 23

Learn More 26

    Coconut Milk Cod en Papillote 27

    Ginger and Mango Chicken en Papillote 29

    Greek Fish en Papillote 31

    Lamb Leg Steaks en Papillote 34

    Mediterranean Salmon and Cauliflower Rice en Papillote 36

    Orange Tarragon Halibut with Smoked Honey en Papillote 39

    Paper Wrapped Lamb with Graviera Cheese, Peas and Carrots 42

Papillote of Seafood 44

Pork Chops en Papillote 47

Pork with Vegetables and Feta en Papillote 49

Salmon and Summer Yellow Squash en Papillote 52

Shrimp, Bok Choy, and Noodles en Papillote 54

Sweet 'n Sour Smoked Tofu and Pineapple en Papillote 58

Turkey and Walnuts En Papillote 61

Sides 64

Broccoli, Asparagus, and Snap Peas en Papillote 65

Corn on the Cob in a Bag 67

Moroccan-Style Veggies 69

Parsnips and Carrots en Papillote 72

Portobello Mushrooms en Papillote 74

Potatoes with Rosemary and Thyme en Papillote 77

Shiitake Mushrooms and Brown Rice in Parchment Paper 79

Sweet Potatoes en Papillote 81

Vegetable Stacks en Papillote 83

Whole Roasted Cauliflower with Garden Herb Sauce 86

Desserts 89

    Apple Cinnamon with Cognac and Red Currants en Papillote 90

    Apple Pie in a Bag 93

    Banana, Honey, Pistachio and Ginger en Papillote 97

    Blueberry, Peach, and Almonds en Papillote 99

    Goat Cheese and Pear Papillote with Sweet Yogurt Sauce 101

    Honeyed Plums en Papillote 104

    Peaches in Paper with Homemade Basil Ice Cream 106

    Red Berry Medley en Papillote 110

    Rhubarb-Strawberry en Papillote 112

    Tropical Papillote of Mango, Coconut, and Banana 114

Author's Afterthoughts 116

About the Author 117

Introduction

It may sound fancy but preparing meals en papillote is a lot easier than you may think. From meals for one to family-size servings, dinner in a bag is ideal for anyone looking for a low-prep and quick clean-up meal.

In cooking, the term en papillote means cooking food in paper or in parchment. Here, the food is enclosed inside a packet, bag or parcel of paper and cooked in the oven. It's the perfect way to cook meat, seafood, and veggies as it helps the protein retain their juices and the veggies their valuable nutrients.

Along with the protein in the packet, you can add herbs, spices, seasonings, citrus juices, wine, and more. The parcel contents give off steam, which cooks the food, and in no time at all, you have dinner in a bag!

What's more, if you aren't up to creating your own parcels, you can invest in some pre-cut parchment paper cooking bags.

From apple pie in a bag to honeyed plums en papillote, if you are looking to impress, the French cooking method is ideal for preparing savory dishes and even sweet desserts too.

So, what are you waiting for? Dinner is in a bag!

Mains

Bacon-Wrapped Rabbit en Papillote

As the most exercised part of a rabbit, rabbit legs can be tough when not cooked properly. However, the meat prepared en papillote will stay moist, tender, and juicy. Better yet, this dish is healthy too!

Servings: 6

Total Time: 50mins

Ingredients:

- 1 tbsp fresh tarragon (minced and divided)
- 1¾ ounce Gruyere cheese (grated and divided)
- 6 rabbit legs
- 12 smoked bacon slices
- Freshly ground black pepper

Directions:

Preheat the main oven to 350 degrees F.

Lay the parchment paper on a clean worktop.

Add half of the minced tarragon and half of the grated cheese.

Wrap each rabbit leg with 2 slices of bacon.

Arrange the bacon-wrapped rabbit legs on the parchment paper, scatter over the remaining minced tarragon and grated Gruyere, and season with pepper.

Wrap the paper around the mixture, securing with twine, to seal.

Bake in the preheated oven for 45 minutes, until cooked through.

Serve and enjoy.

Beef in Parchment with Olive Sauce

Uncork the red wine, set the table, and get ready to unwrap and enjoy this tender beef and olive main.

Servings: 6

Total Time: 1hour 15mins

Ingredients:

- 1 (2½ pounds) center-cut beef fillet
- 3 tbsp extra-virgin olive oil (divided)
- Salt and freshly ground black pepper
- ½ cup shallots (minced)
- ¾ cup niçoise olives (pitted and divided)
- 1 large rosemary sprig
- ½ cup dry red wine
- 1 tbsp Dijon mustard
- Rosemary sprigs (to garnish)

Directions:

Preheat the main oven to 400 degrees F.

Rub the beef all over with 1 tablespoon of olive oil and season with salt and freshly ground black pepper.

Securely wrap in a large piece of parchment paper and using butcher's twine tie like a parcel at the top.

Transfer the parcel to a baking dish and roast until medium-rare doneness for approximately 30 minutes. When 25 minutes have elapsed, insert a meat thermometer into the center of the beef, cutting through the paper. The meat is good to go when it registers between 120-125 degrees F.

Remove the beef from the oven, and while still wrapped, place on a chopping board to rest for 30-60 minutes.

While the meat roasts, in a skillet, heat the remaining 2 tablespoons of oil.

Add the shallots to the pan and on moderate to low heat, sauté until soft and starting to just color.

Finely chop half of the pitted olives and add them to the pan, followed by the sprig of rosemary. Stir well to combine, and pour in the red wine, cooking for 2-3 minutes over moderate heat, until the mixture starts to reduce.

Next, stir in the Dijon mustard and add the remaining whole olives. Remove the pan from the heat.

Once the meat has rested for a minimum of 30 minutes, remove the string from the paper parcel and open it carefully to retain the juices.

Using kitchen tongs, carefully lift the meat from the paper. Pour the meat juices from the parchment into the pan containing the sauce.

Simmer the sauce for 4-5 minutes, until just thickened. Season with salt and black pepper and slice the meat to a ½" thickness.

Arrange the meat on a platter, garnish with rosemary sprigs and serve the sauce, warm on the side.

Catfish en Papillote

Catfish is a meaty and juicy fish and holds its shape well when prepared in paper. Here, topped with garden herbs and cooked in white wine and clam juice, it makes a flavorful midweek meal for two.

Servings: 2

Total Time: 25mins

Ingredients:

- 2 celery ribs (cut into 3" pieces, then into long strips)
- 1 large carrot (peeled and cut into 3" pieces, then into long strips)
- ¼ cup olive oil (to brush)
- 1 red onion (peeled and sliced)
- 2 catfish fillets
- 3 tbsp dry white wine
- Freshly squeezed juice of 1 lemon
- 2 tbsp clam juice
- 1 large tomato (seeded and chopped)
- 2 tbsp fresh parsley (chopped)
- 1 tsp fresh thyme leaves
- 1 tsp fresh dill (chopped)
- 1 tsp fresh tarragon (chopped)
- ½ tsp sea salt
- ½ tsp ground black pepper

Directions:

Preheat the main oven to 400 degrees F.

Bring a small pan of water to a boil, add the celery and carrots and cook for 60 seconds. Remove the veggies from the pan, place them in a bowl, and rinse under cold running water. Pat the veggies dry with a kitchen paper towel.

Cut 2 sheets of parchment paper into 20" squares. Fold in half and crease lightly. Unfold the parchment paper, and brush lightly on one side of each sheet with olive oil.

Divide the celery, carrots, and raw red onion slices evenly into small piles on one half of each parchment sheet.

Lay one catfish fillet on top of the veggies on each sheet. Fold up the edges of the parchment paper lightly to make a boat-shape.

In a bowl, combine the white wine with the fresh lemon juice and clam juice.

Drizzle each catfish fillet with 3 tablespoons of the mixture, ensuring it is contained within the paper.

Spoon half of the chopped tomatoes over each catfish fillet, and scatter half of the fresh herbs (parsley, thyme, dill, and tarragon) over the top. Season the mixture with sea salt and black pepper.

Fold the paper over the catfish fillets and veggies.

Starting at the creased corner, begin folding the edges over by ½ ". Continue until the paper is a series of tight and overlapping folds.

Transfer the parcels to a large baking sheet, and bake in the oven for 10-12 minutes until the bags are puffing up and slightly browned.

Champagne and Orange Lobster Tails en Papillote

Are you feeling fancy? Then, look no further than these champagne and orange steamed lobster tails. They are ready from paper to plate in just 60 minutes.

Servings: 4

Total Time: 1hour

Ingredients:

- 8 fresh orange slices
- ¼ cup fennel fronds (chopped)
- ¾ cup dry champagne
- 4 (5 ounces) lobster tails
- 2 tbsp butter (cut into small pieces)
- ¼ tsp sea salt

Directions:

Preheat the main oven to 425 degrees F. Prepare 4 (15x24") pieces of parchment paper. Fold the paper crosswise, in half. Draw a large half-size heart shape on each piece of paper. The fold should be in the middle of the heart. Cut the heart out, and open up.

Layer 2 slices of orange, 1 lobster tail, 1½ teaspoons of butter, and 1 tablespoon of fennels fronds close to the fold of each piece of paper.

Spoon 3 tablespoons of Champagne over each portion.

At the top of the heart shape, fold the parchment paper's edges, sealing the edges with a narrow fold. Secure the end tip, twisting to secure.

Arrange the packets on a sheet pan and bake in the preheated oven for 12 minutes.

Remove from the oven. Then, allow to rest for 5 minutes.

Open the parcels carefully to allow any steam to escape,

Remove the meat from the tails and roughly chop. Return the chopped meat to the shell, and arrange it on a plate.

Drizzle the juices from the paper parcels over each portion of lobster.

Repeat the process until all 4 parcels are ready to serve.

Season with sea salt and enjoy.

Chateaubriand en Papillote

This classic French steak, main for two needs; no introduction and being cooked en papillote, will ensure the meat remains juicy and tender.

Servings: 6

Total Time: 1hour

Ingredients:

- Bordelaise Sauce:
- ¾ cup dry red wine
- 2 medium shallots (finely chopped)
- 1 leaf bay leaf
- ¼ tsp dried thyme
- 2 cups beef stock
- ⅛ tsp salt
- A dash of ground black pepper
- Beef:
- 2 beef fillets
- 3 cups Bordelaise sauce (see recipe)

Directions:

In a small saucepan, prepare the sauce: Combine the red wine with the shallots, bay leaf and thyme.

Over moderate heat, bring to a rolling boil and continue to cook until the contents are reduced in volume by around half.

Pour in the beef stock. Then, bring to boil once more.

With a tablespoon, skim off and remove any surface scum from the sauce.

Continue to cook the sauce until it thickens the back of a spoon. It should be reduced to 75% of its original volume.

Using a fine-mesh sieve, strain the sauce into a bowl. Then, season the sauce to taste with salt and black pepper and use as directed.

For the beef, over moderate heat, broil the fillets until medium-rare for 30 minutes.

Horizontally, cut each beef fillet in half.

Spread the cooled Bordelaise sauce over the bottom half of each beef fillet. Cover the sauce with the top half of the steak, and secure it together.

Place each fillet on a sheet of parchment paper, and brush the paper with olive oil.

Bring the paper up and over to cover the meat.

Preheat the main oven to 450 degrees F.

Transfer to a baking sheet. Then, place in the oven for 3 minutes, or until the paper puffs up.

Carefully unwrap and serve.

Clam Spaghetti en Papillote

While it isn't usual to cook pasta en papillote, it is a great way to produce flavorful spaghetti. The seafood which is steamed in white wine infuses the pasta with flavor.

Servings: 4

Total Time: 55mins

Ingredients:

- 12 ounces spaghetti
- Kosher salt
- 1 tbsp extra-virgin olive oil
- 2 garlic cloves (peeled and sliced)
- 2½ cups store-bought Marinara sauce
- 2 tbsp heavy cream
- 2 tbsp dry white wine
- 16 jumbo shrimps
- 16 Littleneck clams
- 8 ounces skin removed salmon (cut into chunks)
- Red pepper flakes (to season)
- Fresh parsley (chopped, to garnish)
- Parmigiano-Reggiano (freshly grated, to garnish)

Directions:

Preheat the main oven to 425 degrees F.

Bring a large pan of salted water to a boil and cook the spaghetti according to the package directions until al dente, for approximately 7-8 minutes. Drain the pasta well.

Return the cooked pasta to the pan, and over moderate heat, add the oil and the garlic. Cook while stirring until the mixture is beginning to turn into a golden color.

Add the Marinara sauce, heavy cream, and white wine. Stir the mixture to incorporate, and bring to a simmer.

Stir in the cooked and drained spaghetti to combine, and remove the pan from the heat.

Place ¼ of the pasta mixture in the middle of a large sheet of parchment paper.

Top the pasta with ¼ serving each of the shrimp, clams, and salmon. Close the packet and transfer it to a baking sheet. Repeat the process with the remaining 3 portions.

Bake the packets in the oven for 20 minutes or until the seafood is cooked through and the clams open.

Open the packet carefully, season with red pepper flakes, and garnish with chopped parsley and grated cheese.

Learn More

Coconut Milk Cod en Papillote

Cooking fish in coconut milk en papillote will help to lock in the flavors and juices. It is one of the most successful ways of cooking fish, and better yet, it results in very little odor, which is good news if you are hosting a dinner party.

Servings: 4

Total Time: 20mins

Ingredients:

- 4 small zucchinis (finely sliced)
- 3 leeks (trimmed and finely chopped)
- ⅘ cup coconut milk
- 1 tbsp curry powder
- Salt and pink peppercorns
- 4 cod fillets

Directions:

Preheat the main oven to 355 degrees f.

Blanch the zucchini and leeks for 2 minutes.

Divide the veggies between 4 equal-sized parchment paper sheets, placing them in the middle of the paper. Pour over an equal amount of coconut milk, and season with curry powder, salt, and pink peppercorns.

Lay one fresh cod fillet on top of each portion.

Wrap the paper around the mixture to create a parcel, twist the ends to seal, and bake in the preheated oven for 10 minutes.

Serve the fish hot, and enjoy.

Ginger and Mango Chicken en Papillote

The en papillote technique of French cooking steams protein and fruit, which means it takes a tiny amount of oil, making it a healthy option.

Servings: 4

Total Time: 35mins

Ingredients:

- 1 pound skinless boneless chicken breasts
- 1 ripe medium mango (peeled, pitted, and sliced)
- 1 (1") piece ginger (peeled and cut into thin matchsticks)
- 1 jalapeno pepper (finely sliced)
- ⅓ cup fresh cilantro leaves
- 4 tsp avocado oil
- Salt and black pepper
- 1 fresh lime (cut into 8 wedges)

Directions:

Preheat the main oven to 400 degrees F. Prepare 4 (18") pieces of parchment paper.

Fillet the chicken breasts by cutting horizontally in half.

Place ¼ of the mango slices in the middle of each parchment paper piece.

Top with 1 chicken piece, ¼ each of jalapeno and ginger. Season each portion with salt and black pepper, and drizzle each one with 1 teaspoon avocado oil.

Fold the parcels: Pull the paper's sides up and bring them together over the chicken. Then, fold the edges together and down to create several small folds. Twist together tightly to seal.

Place the folded packets on a sheet pan and cook in the preheated oven for 20 minutes.

Unwrap carefully, and serve each portion with 2 wedges of fresh lime.

Greek Fish en Papillote

Season firm white fish fillets with Greek seasoning, cook en papillote with tomatoes, olives, and oregano. Garnish with crumbled feta cheese and enjoy a tasty, moist, Greek-style main dish.

Servings: 2

Total Time: 20mins

Ingredients:

- 1 small red onion (peeled and sliced)
- 2 (4-6 ounces) white fish fillets (of choice)
- 2 tsp Greek seasoning mix
- 2 tbsp Greek extra-virgin olive oil
- 1 fresh lemon (sliced)
- ½ cup cherry tomatoes (halved)
- ½ cup Kalamata olive (halved and pitted)
- 4 fresh oregano sprigs
- Feta cheese (crumbled, to serve)

Directions:

Preheat the main oven to 375 degrees F.

Evenly distribute the onion slices between 2 large parchment paper squares. Place the onion on the right half of each square. Allow approximately 1" of space between the onions and the paper's edge.

Next, lay a fish fillet on top of the onion, and season with the Greek seasoning mix. Drizzle each portion of fish with 1 tablespoon of olive oil.

Arrange half of the lemon slices on top of each portion of fish. Next, place the cherry tomato halves and olives around the outside of the fish. Lay two sprigs of oregano over the top of each fillet.

Fold the left side of one piece of paper over the fish. Fold the paper together, around the edges in ¼ folds to make a half-moon shape. Press, crimp, and fold to make sure the packets are well sealed.

Place the two packets on a sheet pan, and bake in the preheated oven for 8-12 minutes.

Then, remove from the oven, and allow to cool for a few minutes.

Unwrap carefully at the table, scatter over the crumbled feta cheese and enjoy.

Bottom of Form

Lamb Leg Steaks en Papillote

Here, *lamb* leg steaks are wrapped in individual parchment paper packets and cooked with herbs and white wine and cooked until tender.

Servings: 4

Total Time: 40mins

Ingredients:

- 1 tbsp olive oil
- 2 pounds bone-in lamb leg steaks
- 1 small red onion (peeled and thinly sliced)
- 2 garlic cloves (peeled and finely chopped)
- 1 tsp dried oregano
- Sea salt
- 1 tsp cracked black pepper
- 4 fresh bay leaves
- ⅘ cup dry white wine

Directions:

Preheat the main oven to 395 degrees F.

Cut 4 (16") circles out of parchment paper. Rub each circle with a drop of oil.

Place a lamb steak on one half, and scatter over the onion, garlic, dried oregano, and season with salt and pepper.

Top with a bay leaf, and fold in half to create a semi-circle. Fold the edges over to seal. Before you seal the parcels, add a splash of white wine, and complete the folding to ensure the lamb steaks are sealed entirely.

Arrange the parcels on a baking sheet. Then, bake in the preheated oven for 30 minutes.

Unwrap carefully, and enjoy.

Mediterranean Salmon and Cauliflower Rice en Papillote

All of the flavors of the Mediterranean come together in one parcel. What's more, this salmon main made using cauliflower rice is a healthy option for anyone watching or managing their weight.

Servings: 4

Total Time: 40mins

Ingredients:

- 2 tbsp freshly squeezed lemon juice
- 1 tsp lemon zest
- 2 tsp garlic (peeled and minced)
- 1 tsp olive oil
- Red pepper flakes
- 1 fennel bulb (finely sliced)
- 8 Kalamata olives (pitted and sliced)
- ¼ cup red onion (peeled and finely sliced)
- 2 cups cauliflower (shredded)
- 4 (6 ounces) boneless, skinless salmon fillets
- 8 lemon slices

Directions:

Preheat the main oven to 400 degrees F.

In a bowl, combine the fresh lemon juice with the lemon zest, garlic, olive oil, and a pinch of red pepper flakes.

In a larger bowl, toss the fennel with the olives, red onion, and fresh lemon juice mixture.

Cut 4 (12x16") pieces of parchment paper and fold each one in half.

Open the paper. Arrange a ¼ of the cauliflower rice, 1 fillet of salmon, and ¼ of the fennel mixture in the middle of the top half of each piece of paper. Season the mixture liberally with salt and pepper. Top each portion with 2 lemon slices.

Fold the bottom half of the parchment paper over the fish and vegetables. Begin folding and crimping the ends of the paper together, working from one end, all the way around, to the opposing end. You are aiming to create an envelope shape. Fold the end neatly under the envelope to encase the mixture.

Arrange the packets on a sheet pan, and bake in the oven for 25 minutes.

Remove from the oven, unwrap carefully, and enjoy.

Orange Tarragon Halibut with Smoked Honey en Papillote

It's the homemade orange tarragon butter that will add pizzazz to mild, sweet-tasting halibut.

Servings: 4

Total Time: 45mins

Ingredients:

Compound Butter:

- 1 cup unsalted butter (room temperature)
- 2 tbsp orange tarragon
- 1 tbsp fresh parsley (minced)
- 1 tbsp fresh tarragon (minced)
- 1 tbsp fresh orange zest
- ¼ tsp sea salt
- 1 tsp freshly ground Indian coriander

Fish:

- 4 (6 ounces) halibut fillets
- 2 tbsp smoked honey
- 4 tbsp orange tarragon compound butter (see recipe)
- Orange slices (to garnish)

Directions:

First, prepare the compound butter: In a bowl, using a fork, mash the butter until smooth, a little fluffy. Add the remaining ingredients (orange tarragon, fresh parsley, tarragon, orange zest, salt, and coriander. Stir to combine, taste and season.

Cut 2 pieces of kitchen wrap to a length of 12".

In spoonfuls, drop the butter mixture along the middle of each length to form a log-shape. Fold the kitchen wrap over, and press the butter gently into an even, smooth log approximately 1½ "in diameter.

Wrap the logs tightly and twist the ends to compress.

Transfer to the fridge and use as and when directed. The butter can be stored in the fridge for up to 7 days.

For the halibut: Preheat the main oven to 400 degrees F.

Prepare 4 pieces of parchment paper (one for each fillet of fish).

Place the parchment paper sheets on a baking sheet.

Lay a fillet of fish on each sheet of paper and top with 1½ teaspoons honey and 1 tablespoon of orange tarragon compound butter.

Seal the paper packets and place the baking sheet in the oven.

Cook the fish for 12-14 minutes until the paper has puffed up and the fish juices sizzle.

Open the parcels carefully, garnish with slices of orange and serve.

Paper Wrapped Lamb with Graviera Cheese, Peas and Carrots

Graviera cheese comes in second only to feta on the top list of cheeses in Greece. It's a hard cheese with a light to deep yellow color and lends itself perfectly for this paper-wrapped lamb dish.

Servings: 6

Total Time: 2hours 15mins

Ingredients:

- 5¼ ounces butter
- 1 (3 pounds) leg of lamb (chopped into 6 pieces)
- 3 large carrots (peeled and sliced into rounds)
- 1 cup peas
- 8 ounces Graviera cheese (cut into cubes)
- 2 tbsp oregano
- Salt and freshly ground black pepper

Directions:

In a small pan, heat the butter.

In a bowl, combine the meat with carrots, peas, and cheese.

To the bowl, add the oregano, salt, and pepper and mix thoroughly.

Pour the melted butter from Step 1, and mix well.

On a clean, flat work surface, lay out 2 sheets of parchment paper on top of one another.

Spoon the contents of the bowl onto the paper, and fold to create a large-size pouch. Tie the pouch with kitchen twine and wrap it with foil. Transfer to the oven for 2-3 hours.

Remove from the oven, discard the foil and serve the lamb from the inner paper parcel.

Papillote of Seafood

Seafood fans will love this cooking method. Not only will it lock-in all of the briny juices and flavors, but it won't also fill the house with any unwanted fishy smells.

Servings: 2

Total Time: 35mins

Ingredients:

- Olive oil (as needed)
- 1 red onion (peeled, halved, and cut into thin wedges)
- 2 baby fennel bulbs (diagonally and finely sliced)
- 2 spring onions (diagonally and finely sliced)
- 1 lemongrass stalk (diagonally and finely sliced)
- 2 whole star anises (divided)
- 1 thumb fresh ginger (peeled and thinly sliced)
- A small handful of fresh coriander (coarsely chopped)
- 1 garlic clove (peeled and finely chopped)
- Salt and freshly ground black pepper
- 1½ pounds mussels (scrubbed)
- 5 ounces fresh raw tiger prawns
- 3-4 ounces dry white wine
- 3-4 tbsp full-fat coconut milk

Directions:

Preheat the main oven to 425 degrees F. Prepare 2 (12x16") sheets of parchment paper.

In a large pan, heat a splash of olive oil. Add the onion, fennel, spring onions, ginger, lemongrass, star anise, ginger, and coriander. Cook over high heat, while tossing, for 3 minutes, until the veggies start to soften.

Add the garlic to the pan, and season to taste.

Next, stir in the mussels, followed by the prawns and splash of white wine. The wine should moisten and not drown the ingredients.

Cover the pan with a lid. Then, cook for 30-60 seconds.

Remove the pan from the heat and check that the mussels are open. If not, return to the heat for 2-3 seconds until they are.

Using a slotted spoon, scoop the mussels and veggies into a bowl.

Pour the coconut milk into the pan. Match the quantity of milk with the juice in the pan. Boil for approximately 4 minutes until the mixture is a syrup-like jus consistency.

Return the mussels and veggies to the pan, drizzle with oil and shake, to combine.

Take one sheet of parchment paper, and push it into a deep pan.

Spoon in half of the cooked mussels and veggies and one star anise. Lift the paper out carefully, and twist at the top to create a beggar's purse.

Tie the purse tightly with twine, and make the second beggar's purse.

Place the purses in a roasting pan, and place in the oven for 3-4 minutes until the papers start to scorch.

Lift the bags carefully out, untie and serve.

Pork Chops en Papillote

Give everyday pork chops a makeover with a tasty topping and cook in paper for maximum juice retention.

Servings: 3

Total Time: 1hour 40mins

Ingredients:

- 1 pound pork chops
- Salt and freshly ground black pepper
- 2 large red onions (peeled and grated)
- 2 tbsp parsley (minced)
- 2 eggs (hardboiled, shelled, and minced)

Directions:

First, season the chops on both sides with salt and freshly ground black pepper. Put to one side.

Second, cut parchment paper to the same size as the chops while allowing a 2" border all the way around.

In a bowl, combine the grated onion with the minced parsley and minced egg.

Coat each pork chop with an even amount of the onion mixture, and place on one side of the parchment paper.

Next, fold the other side of the paper over. Crimp, and fold the edges to create an empanada shape and to seal.

Repeat the process until the chops are wrapped.

Transfer to a sheet pan, and bake in the oven for 350 degrees F, for approximately 90 minutes.

Unwrap, serve and enjoy.

Pork with Vegetables and Feta en Papillote

Pork shoulder cooked in paper is the best way to make sure the meat is tender and moist. And with fresh veggies and salty feta cheese, rest assured it makes a restaurant-worthy main.

Servings: 6-8

Total Time: 4hours 20mins

Ingredients:

- 1½ pounds pork shoulder (rinsed, patted dry, and cut into bite-size pieces)
- 4 tbsp olive oil (divided)
- 1 tbsp freshly squeezed lemon juice
- Salt and black pepper
- A handful of thyme
- 2 tbsp butter
- 2 carrots (rinsed and sliced)
- 3 waxy variety potatoes (peeled and coarsely chopped)
- 2 red bell peppers (halved, seeded, membrane removed, and diced)
- 1 small zucchini (rinsed, dried, cut lengthwise in half, and sliced)
- 2 garlic cloves (peeled and chopped)
- 5 ounces feta cheese (divided into 4)

Directions:

Preheat the main oven to 350 degrees F.

Add the pork shoulder to a bowl, followed by 2-3 tablespoons of oil. Then, season the meat with freshly squeezed lemon juice, salt, and black pepper.

Rinse the thyme, gently dry to shake, and put half of the stalks to one side. Pluck off any remaining leaves from the thyme and add to the pork mixture. Cover and allow to stand for 3 hours.

Next, cut out 4 large pieces of parchment paper.

Heat the butter in a frying pan. Add the carrots and potatoes to the pan and on moderate heat, sauté for 8-10 minutes, until tender.

Add the bell peppers, zucchini, and garlic and briefly sauté. Then, remove the pan from the heat and season to taste with salt and black pepper.

In a second frying pan, heat the remaining oil.

Next, add the pork to the pan, and sear all over.

Divide the veggies and pork between the 4 pieces of parchment paper.

Top each portion with a piece of feta, thyme sprigs, and season with salt and black pepper.

Fold the paper tightly and tie the parcels using twine or secure with toothpicks.

Arrange the parcels in a casserole dish and bake in the preheated oven for 60 minutes.

Remove the parcels from the oven, unwrap and serve.

Salmon and Summer Yellow Squash en Papillote

Zucchini and summer squash are quick-cooking veggies, which is good news when you don't have much time to spend cooking. Cooking this fish dish en papillote also means there is minimal clean-up required.

Servings: 2

Total Time: 25mins

Ingredients:

- 1 zucchini (cut lengthwise into ⅛" slices)
- 1 summer yellow squash (cut lengthwise into ⅛" slices)
- ¼ cup green onions, white and light green portions (thinly sliced)
- 1½ tsp fresh thyme leaves
- Kosher salt and freshly ground pepper
- 2 (6 ounces, 1½") thick salmon fillets
- ½ lemon (sliced into fine rounds)
- 1 tbsp unsalted butter (cubed)

Directions:

In a bowl, toss the zucchini with the green onions, squash, and thyme. Season the mixture with salt and black pepper.

Make ready 2 (½ sheets) of parchment paper. Each one 12x16" and place on a clean work surface.

Spoon half of the veggie mixture into the middle of each sheet. Lay a salmon filet on top. Then, season with salt and pepper and garnish with slices of lemon.

Dot with cubes of butter, and enjoy.

Shrimp, Bok Choy, and Noodles en Papillote

If you are craving an Asian-inspired meal but watching your weight, then this shrimp, bok choy, and noodle dish is the way to go!

Servings: 2

Total Time: 30mins

Ingredients:

- 2 portions Asian noodles (cooked, drained, and slightly cooled)

Sauce:

- 3 tbsp soy sauce
- 3 tbsp rice vinegar
- 2 tbsp freshly squeezed lime juice
- 2 tbsp hoisin sauce
- 2 tbsp Asian chili garlic
- 3 garlic cloves (peeled and minced)
- 2 tsp fresh ginger (peeled and minced)

Shrimp:

- 6 baby bok choy (thick end trimmed, rinsed, and into ½ "slices)
- 16-20 raw shrimps (peeled and deveined)
- 2 green onions (pale green and white parts only, thinly sliced)
- Fresh cilantro (chopped, to garnish)
- Lime Wedges (to serve)

Directions:

Preheat the main oven to 375 degrees F. Position a rack in the middle of the oven.

Prepare the noodles according to the package directions. Then, drain and cool.

In the meantime, prepare the sauce. Then, in a small bowl, combine all the ingredients (soy sauce, rice vinegar, freshly squeezed lime juice, hoisin sauce, Asian chili garlic, garlic, and ginger). Mix thoroughly to combine.

Add the prepared shrimp to a bowl.

Add the bok choy to a second bowl.

Add the cooled noodles to a third bowl.

Evenly divide the sauce between the 3 bowls, and toss to evenly and well coat. Set aside to rest while you prepare the parchment paper.

Make ready 2 (15x24") pieces of parchment paper. Fold each piece in half to create 15x12" pieces.

With the fold perpendicular to you and on the right-hand side, take a pan, and draw out half a heart shape. Begin from the bottom of the folded side, up and back to the folded edges around 3-4" from the top.

Repeat the process with the remaining parchment paper.

Using scissors, cut along the drawn line, and open up so that the fold is in the middle of the heart. Brush the inside with oil, leaving 2" around the outside oil-free.

To assemble the packets, place a mound of noodles on one side of the heart, in a line and close the paper fold.

Top with half of the bok choy followed by 8-10 shrimp.

Repeat the process with the remaining piece of paper.

Top each one with green onions before dividing any remaining sauce over the top of the shrimp.

To seal the packets, fold the empty half of the heart shape to meet the other side evenly.

Beginning at the top of the folded edge, start to pleat and pinch and press down to seal as you make your way around the edges. At the bottom, twist to seal.

Arrange the parcels on a sheet pan, and bake in the oven for 12-15 minutes until the paper puffs up.

When the shrimp are sufficiently cooked through, take a sharp knife and make a slit from the top to the bottom of the parcel.

Garnish with cilantro and serve with wedges of lime for squeezing.

Sweet 'n Sour Smoked Tofu and Pineapple en Papillote

Cooking tofu en papillote with seasoned rice, Asian seasoning, and fresh pineapple will help this dish absorb all the different flavors.

Servings: 4

Total Time: 35mins

Ingredients:

- 1 cup basmati rice
- 1 (10 ounces) package frozen spinach
- ½ tsp low-sodium soy sauce
- ½ tsp toasted sesame seeds
- 2 tsp chili sauce
- 2 ½ tsp toasted sesame oil (divided)
- 1 (6 ounces) package baked smoked tofu (diced)
- 1 cup fresh pineapple (peeled, cored, and diced)

Directions:

Preheat the main oven to 400 degrees F. Prepare 4 (15") lengths of parchment paper and fold each length in half. Put to one side.

Cook the rice and spinach in separate pans and according to the package instructions. Transfer the rice to a bowl. Then, stir in 1½ teaspoons of sesame oil and the sesame seeds.

Drain the spinach, squeeze out any excess liquid and stir in the soy sauce.

Open up the parchment paper sheets, as you would a book. Arrange ½ cup of cooked basmati on one side of the crease on each sheet.

Top the basmati rice with a ¼ cup each of the following ingredients: smoked tofu, spinach, and pineapple.

Drizzle each serving with ¼ teaspoon of sesame oil and ½ teaspoon chili sauce.

Fold the parchment paper over the foods so that the edges meet. Crimp and seal the parcels with a small, overlapping, and diagonal fold.

Place the parcels on a rimmed baking sheet. Then, bake in the preheated oven for 10 minutes. Set aside to cool for 2 minutes before serving.

Turkey and Walnuts En Papillote

This turkey main course, cooked en papillote with dried fruit and nuts, makes the ideal weekend meal.

Servings: 4

Total Time: 1hour

Ingredients:

- ¼ cup Dijon mustard
- ⅛ cup California walnuts (finely chopped)
- 1 tbsp fresh rosemary (chopped)
- 1 tbsp fresh sage (chopped)
- ¼ tsp black pepper
- 4 (4 ounces) turkey cutlets (about 4 ounces each), all visible fat removed
- 2 leeks, white part only (cut crosswise into thin slices)
- 1 medium zucchini (cut crosswise into ¼ "slices)
- 1 medium yellow squash (cut crosswise into ¼ "slices)
- ¼ cup California walnuts (coarsely chopped)
- 2 tsp grated lemon zest

Directions:

Preheat the main oven to 375 degrees F. Fold 4 (12") sheet of parchment paper, crosswise in half. Then, cut each piece into a heart shape, trimming very close to the paper's edger to use a much paper as you can.

In a bowl, combine the mustard with the finely chopped walnuts, fresh rosemary, fresh sage, and black pepper. Put the bowl to one side.

On a flat work surface or chopping board, for each parcel, place a turkey cutlet on one side of the paper heart. Brush the surface of the turkey with the mustard and walnut mixture.

Add ¼ of the leeks to each pork cutlet.

Place the zucchini and squash on top of the leeks. Scatter each portion with 1 tablespoon of coarsely chopped walnuts along with ½ teaspoon of grated lemon zest.

Fold the remaining half of the paper over the mixture.

To seal the parcels, beginning at the rounded end, roll the parchment paper edges together to approximately ¼ "towards the middle. Continue making your way around the parcel to the bottom, twisting to close and seal.

Lay the parcels on a baking sheet, and bake in the oven for 25-30 minutes until the veggies are tender and the turkey cooked through.

Transfer the parcels to individual plates, open them carefully and enjoy.

Sides

Broccoli, Asparagus, and Snap Peas en Papillote

Cooking fresh green veggies in paper is the perfect way to bring out their fresh flavor. What's more, it means no cleaning of pots and pans.

Servings: 4

Total Time: 15mins

Ingredients:

- 1½ cups small broccoli florets
- 6 ounces asparagus (cut into 2" lengths)
- 1¼ cups sugar snap peas (trimmed)
- 1 tbsp unsalted butter
- 1 tsp grainy prepared mustard
- Coarsely ground salt and black pepper

Directions:

Preheat the main oven to 400 degrees F.

Add the broccoli florets, asparagus, sugar snap peas, butter, and mustard to the middle of a 24" long sheet of parchment paper. Season the veggies with salt and black pepper. Then, fold the parchment into an envelope shape.

Lay the envelope on a baking pan or sheet and cook in the oven until the paper is puffed up and the veggies just tender. This process will take 10-12 minutes.

Carefully unwrap and serve.

Corn on the Cob in a Bag

Who doesn't love corn on the cob? It's the ideal side dish for grilled meats, burgers, ribs, and more.

Servings: 4

Total Time: 15mins

Ingredients:

- 4 ears corn (husked and silk removed)
- 2 tbsp butter
- Sea salt and freshly ground black pepper

Directions:

Place each corn ear in the center of a large sheet of parchment paper. Dot each ear with ½ teaspoon of butter, and season with sea salt and black pepper.

Fold the parchment paper over the corn and seal the packet with crimped folds. First folding across their length and then across their width.

Cook the corn at 350 degrees F for 10 minutes, flip over and cook for an additional 10 minutes.

Serve and enjoy.

Moroccan-Style Veggies

Vegetables, herbs, and spiced cooked en papillote are an easy, healthy, and flavorful way to prepared seasoned root vegetables.

Servings: 4

Total Time: 45mins

Ingredients:

- 1½ pounds sweet potatoes (cubed)
- 6 turnips (trimmed and halved)
- 2 celery stalks (trimmed and thinly sliced)
- 1 onion (peeled and cut into wedges)
- ½ cup raisins
- 1 cup vegetable broth
- ½ tsp turmeric
- ½ tsp ginger
- ½ tsp cinnamon
- 8 red pepper slices
- 4 fresh lemon slices
- 8 tbsp fresh parsley (chopped)
- 8 tbsp cilantro
- 4 tbsp butter

Directions:

In a bowl, combine the sweet potatoes, turnips, celery, onion, and raisins. Pour in the vegetable broth and season with turmeric, ginger, and cinnamon. Stir to combine and moisten.

Scoop ¼ of the veggie mixture into the center of 1 sheet of parchment paper. Top with 2 slices of red pepper, 1 slice of lemon, 2 tablespoons parsley, 2 tablespoons cilantro, and 1 tablespoon of butter.

Fold the parchment to create an envelope shape. Repeat the process with the remaining ingredients to create 4 envelopes in total.

Place the envelopes on a baking sheet and bake in the oven at 400 degrees F for 35-40 minutes, until the vegetables are fork-tender.

Serve and enjoy.

Parsnips and Carrots en Papillote

Sweet maple syrup and dry white wine add a twist to these colorful vegetables prepared in parchment paper.

Servings: 6

Total Time: 40mins

Ingredients:

- 12 ounces parsnips (peeled and cut into thick batons)
- 12 ounces carrots (peeled and cut into thick batons)
- 2 tbsp olive oil
- 1 tbsp unsalted butter (melted)
- 1 tbsp maple syrup
- 1 tbsp + fresh thyme (chopped)
- A splash of dry white wine
- Sea salt and black pepper

Directions:

Preheat the main oven to 425 degrees F. Line a baking sheet with parchment paper.

Add the parsnips and carrots to a bowl followed by the olive oil, butter, maple syrup, 1 tablespoon thyme, and a splash of wine. Season the veggies with salt and black pepper.

Mound the veggies loosely in the middle of a sheet of parchment paper on a baking sheet.

Fold the parchment paper, up and over the veggies, in the middle, and at the edges. Seal the parcel to prevent any steam from escaping.

Bake the vegetables in the oven, until crisp-tender, for approximately 25-30 minutes.

Remove from the oven, unwrap carefully, and garnish with additional chopped thyme.

Portobello Mushrooms en Papillote

Mushrooms cooked using the en papillote method allow themselves to cook but not brown, and this side dish is the perfect partner to fish or poultry mains.

Servings: 4-6

Total time: 35mins

Ingredients:

- 1 tbsp unsalted butter (melted)
- 1 pound Portobello mushrooms (wiped clean and chopped into bite-sized pieces)
- ½ tsp sea salt
- ¼ tsp freshly ground black pepper
- 1 tbsp unsalted butter (chopped into small pieces)
- 1 tsp freshly squeezed lemon juice
- 2 tbsp fresh flat-leaf parsley (chopped)

Directions:

Preheat the main oven to 375 degrees F.

Make an 18x11" rectangle out of parchment paper and fold the rectangle crosswise in half. Open the paper and brush with a light coating of melted butter. Place the paper, the greased side facing upwards on a rimmed baking sheet.

Add the chopped mushrooms to a bowl. Season the mushroom with ½ teaspoon of salt and ¼ teaspoon of black pepper. Add the pieces of butter along with the fresh lemon juice and chopped parsley. Toss the ingredients to combine.

Spread the mushroom mixture over 1 half of the parchment paper. Fold the remaining half of the paper rectangle over the mixture and fold the vertical edges over twice. Work your way to the edge of the parchment paper to the end, and twist to seal.

Arrange the parchment parcel on a rimmed baking sheet.

Place the baking sheet in the preheated oven and cook for approximately 15 minutes, or until the paper is puffed up and the mushrooms cooked.

Unwrap the parcel carefully and serve.

Potatoes with Rosemary and Thyme en Papillote

Rosemary and thyme provide the perfect seasoning for this potato parchment-paper side.

Servings: 4

Total Time: 35mins

Ingredients:

- 1 pound (1-2" diameter) baby red potatoes (cut into ½ "thick rounds)
- 1 pound (1-2" diameter) Yukon Gold potatoes (cut into ½ "thick rounds)
- 2 tbsp olive oil
- 2 tbsp shallot (finely chopped)
- 2 tsp fresh rosemary (chopped)
- 1 tsp fresh thyme (chopped)
- Sea salt and black pepper

Directions:

Preheat the main oven to 375 degrees F. Place 2 (12x16") sheets of parchment paper, side by side, on a clean work surface.

In a bowl, toss both varieties of potatoes, baby red and Yukon Gold, with olive oil, shallot, rosemary, thyme, and season with sea salt and black pepper.

Scoop half of the mixture into the middle of each parchment sheet. Bring the longer ends of 1 sheet together in the middle to make a ½ "fold. Make several more ½ "folds to create a tight seal. Twist the ends of the parcel to close entirely.

Place the parcels on a rimmed baking sheet in the preheated oven, and cook for 25-30 minutes or until the potatoes are tender.

Open carefully and enjoy.

Shiitake Mushrooms and Brown Rice in Parchment Paper

These steamed mushrooms are meaty and full of flavor. When paired with healthy brown rice, they will satisfy your taste buds as well as sate your hunger.

Servings: 4

Total Time: 30mins

Ingredients:

- 2 cups cooked brown rice
- 4 cups shiitake mushrooms (thinly sliced)
- 8 fresh thyme sprigs
- Coarsely ground salt and black pepper
- ¼ cup extra-virgin olive oil
- 1 cup fresh greens (to serve)
- 1 lemon (cut into wedges, for squeezing)

Directions:

Preheat the main oven to 425 degrees F. Prepare 4 (12x16") pieces of parchment paper.

Divide the cooked brown rice evenly between each piece of paper.

Top each portion of rice with an equal amount of mushrooms and thyme. Season the mixture with salt, pepper, and a drizzle of oil.

Fold the paper over to create 4 envelope shapes.

Lay the parcels on a baking pan or rimmed baking sheet and cook for 20-25 minutes until the parcels are puffed up, and the mushrooms are cooked through.

Carefully unwrap, and serve each portion with ¼ cup of fresh greens and a squeeze of fresh lemon juice.

Sweet Potatoes en Papillote

SSsAdding a garnish of toasted pecans to these perfectly cooked sweet potatoes will create textures to the already sensational side.

Servings: 4

Total Time: 30mins

Ingredients:

- 2 sweet potatoes (peeled and cubed)
- 16 garlic cloves (whole and unpeeled)
- 1 large onion (peeled and thinly sliced)
- ¼ cup butter
- Salt and black pepper
- 2 tbsp toasted pecans (chopped, to serve)

Directions:

Preheat the main oven to 450 degrees F. Make ready 2 large pieces of parchment paper.

Divide the sweet potato cubes, garlic, onion, and butter into 2 portions. Then, place 1 portion of the mixture in the center of each sheet of paper. Season the veggies with salt and pepper.

Transfer to the oven. Then, cook for 20-25 minutes, until the potatoes are fork-tender.

Serve, garnished with chopped pecans.

Vegetable Stacks en Papillote

They say a *watched pot never boils*, so why wait around until it does! Instead, prepare your vegetable side dishes in the French way, en papillote.

Servings: 2

Total Time: 1hour

Ingredients:

- 1 medium eggplant (peeled and cut into ½" thick slices)
- 1 tsp salt
- Water (as needed)
- 1 onion (peeled and cut into ½" slices)
- Extra-virgin oil
- 1 cup fresh spinach (torn)
- ¼ cup Greek feta (crumbled)
- 1 medium Yukon Gold potato (very finely sliced)
- Salt and freshly ground black pepper
- 1 roasted bell pepper (cut into ½" strips)
- 1 cup Romano cheese (grated)
- 2 beefsteak tomatoes (sliced)
- A sprinkling of dried sage
- A sprinkling of dried oregano

Directions:

Add the eggplant to a bowl. Season with 1 teaspoon of salt, and pour in enough water to entirely cover the eggplant. Stir the water to dissolve the salt. Weigh the eggplant down using a plate, and put to one side until you are ready to prepare the stacks.

Preheat the main oven to 350 degrees F.

Prepare 2 sheets of parchment paper that are both long enough to roll over one veggie stack. You will need enough paper to tie the ends off with kitchen string after closing the pouch.

Drain the eggplant, but do not pat dry

Next, assemble the stacks. For each stack, lay slices of veggies side-by-side in a single row in the center of the paper across its width.

Make the veggie stacks using 3-4 slices of each veggie, with alternating feta, herbs, and oil layers.

A good order to stack is by first selecting slices of onion and then eggplant. Brush the eggplant with oil. Top the stack with half of the spinach and half of the crumbled feta cheese.

Follow with slices of potato. Season the potatoes with salt and pepper. To the stack, add the red pepper and a sprinkling of Romano cheese. Follow this with slices of tomato and a sprinkling of dried sage.

Next are slices of eggplant, a drizzle of olive oil, and a sprinkling of oregano.

Pull the parchment paper carefully around and above the stack. Fold the paper until it nearly touches the veggies and tie each end with string.

Repeat the process to create the second stack.

Add both stacks to a baking sheet and cook in the preheated oven. Cook for 15 minutes before flipping the sheet pan, and cooking for an additional 15 minutes.

Carefully unwrap the stacks, garnish with more grated Romano cheese and enjoy.

Whole Roasted Cauliflower with Garden Herb Sauce

Give a regular cauliflower a culinary makeover by cooking this en papillote and serve with a side of homemade garden herb sauce.

Servings: 8-10

Total Time: 1hour 15mins

Ingredients:

- 1 large head cauliflower
- ¾ cup extra-virgin olive oil (divided)
- Sea salt and black pepper

Sauce:

- ½ cup fresh-leaf parsley
- ½ cup packed fresh cilantro leaves and stems (chopped)
- ½ tsp garlic (peeled and minced)
- 1½ tsp Dijon mustard
- 2 tbsp sherry vinegar
- Sea salt and black pepper

Directions:

Preheat the main oven to 450 degrees F.

Lay the cauliflower on a sheet pan lined with parchment paper.

Brush the cauliflower all over with ¼ cup of olive oil and season with salt and black pepper.

Pull the parchment paper's shorter sides over the cauliflower and fold one end over 2-3 times to seal. Next, fold the long ends of the paper carefully under the cauliflower to make a packet.

Roast the packet on the prepared sheet pan and in the preheated oven for approximately 40 minutes.

Remove from the oven; tear the top of the paper open, and roast for an additional 15-20 minutes.

In a bowl, combine the parsley with cilantro, garlic, Dijon mustard, sherry vinegar, and remaining oil. Then, season with salt and freshly ground black pepper.

Serve the cauliflower warm with a side of sauce.

Desserts

Apple Cinnamon with Cognac and Red Currants en Papillote

Sweet apples with redcurrant jam and brown sugar cooked in Cognac and flavored with warmly spiced cinnamon is a show-stopping booze-infused dessert.

Servings: 4

Total Time: 25mins

Ingredients:

- 4 medium-size Pink Lady or Golden Delicious apples (peeled, cored, and cut in half)
- 4 tbsp redcurrant jam
- A pinch of ground cinnamon
- 1 tbsp brown sugar
- 1 tbsp Cognac
- Fresh redcurrants (as needed)

Directions:

Preheat the main oven to 400 degrees F.

Thinly slice the apples, and arrange them in a circle, overlapping each one until all the slices are used.

Open a store-bought culinary parchment cooking bag; you will need 4 in total.

Lay each bag flat on a clean work surface.

Add 1 tablespoon of redcurrant jam to the center of each bag.

Using a spatula, place the slices of apple on top of the jam.

Scatter a pinch of ground cinnamon and ¼ tablespoon of brown sugar over the top.

Finish by adding ¼ tablespoon of Cognac to each bag's ingredients and scatter with fresh red currants.

Fold each bag 3 times to close, crimp to seal, and bake in the preheated oven for 15 minutes.

Unwrap carefully and serve directly from the bag.

Apple Pie in a Bag

Apple pie is an all-time favorite American and British dessert, but next time you serve it, why not give it a French twist by baking it in paper rather than a dish?

Servings: 10

Total Time: 1hour 20mins

Ingredients:

Bottom Crust:

- 1 cup all-purpose flour
- 1½ tsp white sugar
- 6 tbsp unsalted butter
- 2½ tbsp cold water

Filling:

- 5 pounds Granny Smith apples (peeled, cored, and thinly sliced)
- ½ cup brown sugar
- 2 tbsp all-purpose flour
- 1 tsp ground cinnamon
- ½ tsp ground nutmeg
- A pinch of ground ginger
- 2 tbsp freshly squeezed lemon juice
- 2 tbsp graham cracker crumbs

Topping:

- ½ cup all-purpose flour
- ½ cup butter (softened)
- ½ cup superfine sugar

Directions:

First, prepare the bottom crust. In a bowl, combine the flour with the white sugar until combined.

Rub the unsalted butter into the flour mixture and until it resembles a coarse crumb consistency. Two tablespoons at a time, sprinkle the water over the top. With a metal fork, mix the dough lightly together until it just holds together.

Form the dough into a ball and roll it out to circle approximately ⅛" thick.

Place the dough in an 8" pie dish. Using a knife, cut off any excess pastry.

Finish the edge of the crust using fork tines, and set the crust to one side.

In a bowl, for the filling, combine the apples with the brown sugar, 2 tablespoons of flour, cinnamon, nutmeg, ginger, and fresh lemon juice. Put to one side.

In a bowl, for the topping, combine ½ cup flour with ½ cup of softened butter and sugar to create a moist, sticky dough.

To assemble, cover the bottom of the pie crust with an even and light layer of cracker crumbs.

Fill the pie with the apple mixture, piling it to create a mound.

Pinch pieces of the topping mixture off, and flatten them a little at a time with your fingers. Randomly dot them over the filling to cover as much as is possible.

Preheat the main oven to 425 degrees F.

Take 2 (12x30") pieces of parchment paper.

Place the 2 pieces of paper in an X-shape on a clean work surface.

Place the pie in the middle of the cross, and bring the parchment paper ends up over the pie. Fold and staple the paper over the pie to enclose entirely and seal in the pie. The parchment paper must not touch the pie's top or sides.

Put the paper-wrapped pie on a cookie sheet and bake in the oven for 60 minutes.

Remove the pie from the oven, tear the paper away carefully, and set it aside to cool slightly.

Serve and enjoy.

Banana, Honey, Pistachio and Ginger en Papillote

All it takes is a handful of ingredients, and in no time at all, you can prepare this sweet and sticky dessert.

Servings: 4

Total Time: 20mins

Ingredients:

- 4 bananas (cut lengthwise in half, and then half the on the short length)
- Freshly squeezed juice of 1 lemon
- 4 tsp butter
- ¼ cup clover honey
- 2 tbsp pistachios (chopped)
- 1 tsp orange rind (julienned)
- ½ tsp fresh ginger root (peeled and minced)

Directions:

First, preheat the main oven to 400 degrees F.

Fold 4 sheets of parchment paper in half. Cut out large half-circles along the paper's crease to make full circles, folded in half.

Next, unfold the circles and stuff with 4 pieces of banana, and an equal amount of lemon juice, butter, honey, pistachios, orange rind, and ginger.

Fold the edges back together to create a half-moon shaped pouch.

Crimp and roll the edges to seal or staple.

Then, bake on a baking sheet until heated through, for 3-4 minutes.

Serve direct from the paper.

Blueberry, Peach, and Almonds en Papillote

Tear open these papillote packages and bask in the sweet fragrance of peach, blueberry, and fresh mint.

Servings: 4

Total Time: 40mins

Ingredients:

- 4 ripe peaches (peeled, pitted, sliced into ¼" wedges)
- ¼ cup almond slivers
- ½ cup fresh blueberries
- 1 tbsp + 1 tsp lemon juice
- ¼ cup granulated sugar
- 2 tbsp brown sugar
- 2 tbsp unsalted butter (cut into 4 pieces)
- 12 fresh peppermint leaves (sliced into thin slivers)

Directions:

Preheat the main oven to 400 degrees F. Cut out 4 (13x9") parchment paper rectangles.

Add the peach wedges, almond slivers, and blueberries to a bowl. Toss in the fresh lemon juice and sugars (granulated and brown) until combined.

Divide the fruit mixture between the parchment rectangles, arranging it in a pile just off-center.

Top each pile of fruit with a piece of butter.

Fold the paper over the fruit, creasing and crimping to hold closed.

Transfer the packages to a baking sheet and bake in the oven for 20-25 minutes until puffed up.

Snip open the packages, garnish with fresh mint and serve straight away.

Goat Cheese and Pear Papillote with Sweet Yogurt Sauce

If you're a lover of balancing sweet and savory flavors, you'll adore the way sweet pears complement salty goat cheese in this en papillote recipe. Serve with a delicious and tangy homemade yogurt sauce.

Servings: 4

Total Time: 30mins

Ingredients:

Fruit:

- 2 tbsp olive oil
- 4 ripe pears (peeled, cored, quartered, then cut into thirds)
- Freshly squeezed juice of 1 lemon
- 4 ounces goat cheese (cut into 4 slices)
- 1 tbsp fresh tarragon (chopped)
- Salt

Yogurt Sauce:

- 1 ripe pear (peeled, cored, finely chopped)
- 1 cup plain yogurt
- Freshly squeezed juice of 1 lemon
- Salt

Directions:

Preheat the main oven to 350 degrees F.

Cut 8 large squares of parchment paper.

Brush 4 of the parchment squares with olive oil.

Divide pear thirds between the 4 greased parchment squares, drizzle over the lemon juice, and top with a slice of goat cheese, making sure to leave a 2" border clear.

Scatter over the chopped tarragon and season with a pinch of salt.

Arrange the remaining parchment squares over the fruit and cheese, fold them over the edges to create 4 sealed packets.

Transfer the packets to a baking sheet. Then, bake in the oven for 13-15 minutes.

In the meantime, prepare the sauce. Stir the chopped pear into the yogurt. Then, mix in the lemon juice and season with a small pinch of salt.

When the parcels are baked, take them out of the oven and snip them open.

Serve straight away with a jug of the prepared sweet yogurt sauce on the side.

Honeyed Plums en Papillote

Baking fruit en papillote is the perfect way to seal in all of its delicious juices. In this recipe, plums are elevated to an elegant dessert with bold spices, sweet honey, and crunchy pecans.

Servings: 8

Total Time: 30mins

Ingredients:

- 8 dessert plums (stoned and sliced into thick wedges)
- 1 ounce unsalted butter
- 2 cinnamon sticks (each snapped into 4 smaller pieces)
- 8 whole cloves
- 4 tbsp clear honey
- 1 orange
- 4 scoops vanilla-flavored frozen yogurt
- 3 tbsp pecans (roughly chopped)

Directions:

Preheat the main oven to 400 degrees F.

Cut 8 large squares of parchment paper. Divide the plum wedges between the parchment paper squares and top each with a dot of butter, a piece of cinnamon stick, a clove, and a drizzle of honey.

Zest and juice the orange, then sprinkle the zest and juice over the plums.

Bring the two opposite sides of the parchment over the fruit filling and fold down a few times to seal.

Transfer the packages to a baking sheet and cook in the oven for 20 minutes until the parcels puff up and the fruit mixture is bubbling.

Arrange each parcel on an individual serving plate, snip open and serve with a scoop of frozen yogurt and a sprinkling of chopped pecans.

Peaches in Paper with Homemade Basil Ice Cream

If you don't want to make ice cream, then choose your favorite store-bought flavors; green tea and coconut are both excellent choices.

Servings: 6

Total Time: 9hours 30mins

Ingredients:

Basil Ice Cream:

- 6 egg yolks
- 1 cup heavy cream
- 1 cup milk
- 1 cup packed fresh basil leaves (thick stems removed and divided)
- ⅔ cup granulated sugar

Peaches:

- 6 medium-size ripe peaches (blanched, peeled, pitted, and thinly sliced)
- Freshly squeezed juice of ½ lemon
- 2 tbsp vanilla bean oil
- Sea salt and freshly ground black pepper
- Basil ice cream (see recipe)

Directions:

To prepare the ice cream, add the egg yolks to an electric mixer bowl, and using the whip attachment, on high, whip until fluffy and light. Put to one side.

Make ready an ice bath. You will need this to cool the custard by putting a smaller bowl inside an ice-filled larger bowl. Put to one side.

Over moderate heat, in a pan, combine the heavy cream with the milk and around half of the fresh basil leaves. Bring the mixture to a simmer.

Remove the pan from the heat. Then, set it aside to steep for 10 minutes. In a colander, strain the basil, and remove and discard the leaves. Return the mixture to the pan.

Next, add the sugar to the pan and return the pan to heat. Stir the mixture to dissolve the sugar entirely.

When the mixture comes to a simmer and steam is rising, with a ladle, a little at a time, add some of the hot mixture to the beaten egg yolks. Whisk well to combine, and transfer the egg yolk mixture to the pan.

Continue to cook the mixture over moderate to moderate-low heat, stirring continually using a wooden spoon. The custard is ready when it runs down the back of the spoon.

Take the custard off the heat and add the remaining fresh basil leaves, and with an immersion blender, blend.

Using a fine-mesh strainer, strain the custard into the smaller bowl, set over the larger bowl filled with iced water. Stir well to cool, and once cooled, transfer to a fridge-safe container and place in the fridge for 8 hours.

Next, churn the mixture in your ice cream maker, according to the device manual. Use the ice cream as directed.

For the peaches en papillote: Preheat the main oven to 400 degrees F. Make 4 (10") squares of parchment paper and fold each one in half. Get a good crease along the edges, and cut the squares along the crease into heart-shapes. Put to one side.

Then, in a bowl, toss the peach slices with the fresh lemon juice.

Divide the tossed peach slices between the opened parchment paper hearts. Add the peaches as close to the crease as possible. Fold the other half of the heart shape over. Crimp the edges to seal the parcels, beginning at the rounded top. Twist the end of the heart tightly to seal.

Lay the parcels on a baking sheet. Then, bake in the preheated oven for 12-15 minutes or until the paper is puffed up and browned.

Take the packets out of the oven, and place each one on an individual plate or dish.

Cut each packet open, and drizzle with a dash of oil. Season the peaches with sea salt and freshly ground black pepper and serve with the basil ice cream.

Red Berry Medley en Papillote

This berrylicious en papillote dessert is a perfect dinner-party choice. What's more, the prep takes just 5 minutes, and there is very little clean-up afterward.

Servings: 6

Total Time: 25mins

Ingredients:

- 21 ounces mixed red berries (rinsed and dried)
- 6 cups cane sugar syrup
- 2 limes
- Dark chocolate sauce (to serve, optional)

Directions:

Preheat the main oven to 355 degrees F. Cut 6 even-sized squares of parchment paper.

Wash and dry all of the berries.

Divide the berries between the parchment squares and slowly pour over the sugar syrup.

Grate the lime zest over the berries. Slice the limes in half and squeeze the juice over the berries.

Close the parchment squares and arrange them on a baking sheet. Then, bake the parcels in the oven for 15 minutes.

Carefully unwrap, drizzle with chocolate sauce and serve.

Rhubarb-Strawberry en Papillote

This sweet treat is sophisticated yet straightforward, thanks to a delicate balance of maple syrup, aromatic vanilla seeds, fresh lemon verbena, tangy balsamic vinegar, and red fruits.

Servings: 2

Total Time: 25mins

Ingredients:

- 1 cup strawberries (hulled, and quartered)
- 1 cup rhubarb (sliced into ½" pieces)
- ¼ cup pure maple syrup
- 1 tbsp lemon verbena (minced)
- Seeds of 1 vanilla pod
- Vanilla ice cream (to serve)
- Good-quality balsamic vinegar

Directions:

Preheat the main oven to 425 degrees F.

Combine the quartered strawberries, rhubarb, maple syrup, lemon verbena, and vanilla seeds in a bowl. Transfer the mixture to a parchment bag, fold the over a few times, and crimp to seal.

Arrange the bag on a baking sheet and bake in the oven for 15 minutes.

Take the parcel out of the oven and carefully snip open to allow the steam to escape safely.

Divide the fruit between two serving bowls and serve with a scoop of vanilla ice cream, finish with a drizzle of balsamic vinegar.

Tropical Papillote of Mango, Coconut, and Banana

Transport yourself to the tropics with this delicious blend of exotic fruits and aromatic bay leaves baked en papillote.

Servings: 4

Total Time: 15mins

Ingredients:

- 1 ripe mango (peeled, halved, and thinly sliced)
- 4 ripe bananas (peeled, and halved lengthwise)
- 4 bay leaves (halved lengthwise)
- 2 tbsp fresh coconut chips
- Lime sorbet (scooped, to serve)

Directions:

Preheat the main oven to 450 degrees F. Make ready 4 (12x16) pieces of parchment paper.

Divide the mango slices into 4 even portions. Then, add one portion to the center of each piece of parchment paper.

Arrange 2 banana halves, one ½ on each side of the mango slices on each sheet.

On each portion, arrange 2 laurel halves on top of the mango and finish with a sprinkling of coconut chips.

Close the parchment paper squares and bake in the oven for 10 minutes.

Take out of the oven and serve each portion with a scoop of lime sorbet.

Author's Afterthoughts

thank you

I would like to express my deepest thanks to you, the reader, for making this investment in one my books. I cherish the thought of bringing the love of cooking into your home.

With so much choice out there, I am grateful you decided to Purch this book and read it from beginning to end.

Please let me know by submitting an Amazon review if you enjoyed this book and found it contained valuable information to help you in your culinary endeavors. Please take a few minutes to express your opinion freely and honestly. This will help others make an informed decision on purchasing and provide me with valuable feedback.

Thank you for taking the time to review!

Christina Tosch

About the Author

Christina Tosch is a successful chef and renowned cookbook author from Long Grove, Illinois. She majored in Liberal Arts at Trinity International University and decided to pursue her passion of cooking when she applied to the world renowned Le Cordon Bleu culinary school in Paris, France. The school was lucky to recognize the immense talent of this chef and she excelled in her courses, particularly Haute Cuisine. This skill was recognized and rewarded by several highly regarded Chicago restaurants, where she was offered the prestigious position of head chef.

Christina and her family live in a spacious home in the Chicago area and she loves to grow her own vegetables and herbs in the garden she lovingly cultivates on her sprawling estate. Her and her husband have two beautiful children, 3 cats, 2 dogs and a parakeet they call Jasper. When Christina is not hard at work creating beautiful meals for Chicago's elite, she is hard at work writing engaging e-books of which she has sold over 1500.

Make sure to keep an eye out for her latest books that offer helpful tips, clear instructions and witty anecdotes that will bring a smile to your face as you read!

Made in the USA
Las Vegas, NV
19 April 2025